## Contents

**Anna Jackson**
*Foreword*      vii

**Rhys Feeney**
*soy boy*

    the world is at least fifty percent terrible      3
    overshoot      5
    how to make toast      6
    (re)wilding      7
    bioremediation      8
    the president of the united states of america is crazy      11
    t/w: dsh      13
    roy g. biv      16
    MCMI-III      17
    mariner_1.txt      18
    brutalism      19
    pripyat on a good day      20
    current mood      21
    the great pumpkin war      22
    improvise / adapt / overcome      23
    pull down firmly to start the flow of oxygen      24
    to be stable      25

**Ria Masae**
*What She Sees from Atop the Mauga*

    Native Rivalry
        Saipipi, Savai'i, Samoa      29
        Apia, Upolu, Samoa      30
    Vinyl Sundays A-Track      31

| | |
|---|---|
| Intersection | 32 |
| docket dates | 34 |
| Mā | 35 |
| Vinyl Sundays B-Side | 36 |
| Weekend Idol | 37 |
| Black Days | 38 |
| Chipped China | 39 |
| SkyCity Scraps | 40 |
| There is No Translation for Post-Natal Depression in the Samoan Language | 42 |
| Satellite | 45 |
| Parousia | 46 |
| Jack Didn't Build Here | 48 |
| The Artistry Effect | 50 |
| Maker | 51 |
| My Vā | 52 |
| Prologue | 54 |

**Claudia Jardine**
*The Temple of Your Girl*

*Three Excerpts from 'A Gift to Their Daughters'*
*A Poetic Essay on Loom Weights in Ancient Greece*

| | |
|---|---|
| 1. Introduction | 59 |
| 2. The Importance of Textile Manufacture for the Relationships of Women | 60 |
| 3. The Importance of Textile Manufacture for Making Connections | 61 |
| The Flower Crown of Sulpicia | |
| Sulpicia 3.13 – Etta James | 63 |
| Sulpicia 3.14 – Stevie Nicks | 64 |

# AUP new poets 7

Rhys Feeney
Ria Masae
Claudia Jardine

Edited and with a Foreword
by Anna Jackson

AUCKLAND
UNIVERSITY
PRESS

| | |
|---|---:|
| Sulpicia 3.15 – Katy Perry | 65 |
| Sulpicia 3.16 – Nina Simone | 66 |
| Sulpicia 3.17 – Madonna | 67 |
| Sulpicia 3.18 – Julie Andrews | 68 |
| Ode to Goon | 69 |
| Catullus Drops a Tab | 70 |
| High Functioning | 71 |
| Killers | |
|     I. | 72 |
|     II. | 73 |
| Holiday, then | 74 |
| My Father Dreams of His Father | 75 |
| For the Rose Garden | 76 |
| Things That Spooked the Ancient Romans | |
|     I. | 77 |
|     II. | 79 |
|     III. | 82 |
| Eurydice & the No or *How Eurydice Died of* | |
|     *Negligence and a Phonetic Misunderstanding* | 84 |

*Notes*                                                                       89

*Foreword*

AUP New Poets 7 presents three poets whose work is alert to contemporary anxieties, writing at a time when poetry is taking on an increasingly urgent as well as consolatory role as it is shared on social media, read to friends and followers, and returned to again and again in print form. Rhys Feeney's poetry offers a personal take on global concerns, as he wonders whether to 'drink soymilk from a deforested plantation in brazil / or cowmilk from a waikato farm that runs right into the river'; Ria Masae's work belongs very much to the streets of Auckland, drawing on the energy of spoken-word poetry to present precisely observed scenes lit up with a larger significance; Claudia Jardine presents a selection of poems that look back in time, reminding us in 'Things That Spooked the Ancient Romans' that anxiety itself is nothing new, even as she finds in the classics compelling contemporary resonances.

Rhys Feeney opens his selection 'soy boy' with a poem titled 'the world is at least fifty percent terrible', referencing in turn the poem 'Good Bones' by Maggie Smith, which has been in recent years one of the most shared poems on the internet, typically shared in the wake of tragedy or atrocity. Made up of a series of dilemmas and solutions to problems beyond the scale at which any one person can really get a handle on them, Feeney's poem evokes real feeling with comic precision: 'waking up from a dream abt owning a house / for a moment i think i'm in utopia / or maybe australia / but then i see the little patches of mould on the ceiling / i roll over to check my phone / but i forgot to put it on charge last night bc i was too tired . . .' This is self-aware writing, and the line can be very fine between comedy and tragedy: in 'current mood', worries about breathing out $CO_2$ and the long life of a sushi container give some sort of focus to an amorphous feeling 'that you were wrong', while 'the great pumpkin war' dramatises the difficulty of cutting up a pumpkin. There is a serious undercurrent, though, even to the lightest of the poems, while others take on global politics, mental illness, ecological collapse, prejudice and self-harm with intelligence, honesty and vulnerability.

These are relatable, immediately accessible poems that reward close attention and draw on information from a vast range of sources. Feeney gives us precise statistics on the prevalence of youth self-harm, presents a range of headlines proclaiming Trump to be insane, explains the build-up of DDE and DDT in the body, offers an etymology of toast (from *torrere,* to burn) – you can learn as much from his selection of poetry as you would from reading an encyclopedia. Further googling to fill in any of your own knowledge gaps will make your reading richer: Wikipedia will give you the post-Chernobyl context to deepen your reading of 'Pripyat on a good day', while the metaphorical resonance of 'mariner_1.txt' is more powerful if you know about the missing overbar in the code responsible for the failure of the Mariner 1's rocket guidance system. Feeney writes in a world where the internet is an extension not only of the mind but of the personality, writing using the codes and conventions of social media: the lower-case 'i' that refuses to draw attention to itself with capitalisation; abbreviations and acronyms that assume a shared familiarity (or willingness to look up what you don't know); punctuation with gaps on the page, line breaks, slashes, italics and tildes that the reader is expected to navigate as easily as the tone of a conversation.

The language of Ria Masae's poetry is, in contrast, language as it is heard rather than written, whether she is capturing the rhythms and accents of everyday conversation ('*E suga*, did you hear bout Susana?') or using repetition, rhyme and assonance to give her work the energy and drama that has made it so successful in performance. Masae's selection, 'What She Sees from Atop the Mauga', travels from a *fale* in Samoa to the sorrow-shaded, pulsing streets of Auckland city, full of dancing, lights, torn sleeping bags, high-fashion stores, people talking, thinking, posturing, searching, loving, longing and reaching out. There are memorable characters, sharply observed – a woman who 'hoarses laughter that makes /

the *fetu* tattoos on her breasts jiggle'; the school bully witnessed as he secretly '. . . raised a china cup / to the porcelain doll's / love-heart lips'; a woman peeking through her net curtains at the birthday balloons tied to the letterbox next door as they 'bob like buoys in a quiet ocean'. Masae is alert, too, to the details that bring a landscape or setting into focus: the fruit-lined dirt roads of the remembered islands, the woven *fala* and celebration trestle tables of one kind of Auckland household, the double-glazed windows and security-code gate of another.

These are not neutral observations but observations with a political and ethical charge. Masae's sympathies are with the downtrodden, the poor, the homeless, the unwell, those who might be overlooked by successful go-getters who prefer to 'drown the reality' of dispossession, swimming laps in their private swimming pools. Yet the vision these poems offers is neither bleak nor hopeless, but full of beauty, wonder, complexity, community and creativity. 'The Artistry Effect', a poem with its own artistry of arrangement, considers the work of the weaver and wood-carver, while other poems find artistry in the ways people talk, the homes they build, how they dress and dye their hair, feasts made and shared, parties hosted, nails polished, the rhythm of a dance, the grace of a stance.

There can be an artistry to reading, too, and in 'The Temple of Your Girl', Claudia Jardine finds rhythm and grace in the startling images and unlikely facts recorded in classical texts. Rhythm and grace can be found, too, in the gaps that structure her readings, as text gives way to absence, interpretation gives way to astonishment. If the world of omens presented in 'Things That Spooked the Ancient Romans' seems unfamiliar, continuities are found in other poems between the classical world and the contemporary. The poems of Sulpicia can be reinterpreted in the voices of modern singers from Nina Simone to Stevie Nicks; the sparrow poems of Catullus come to life in a new way when Catullus drops a tab; in 'Ode to Goon' a very contemporary scene of drunken love-making amongst broken biscuits is full of details suggestive of the classical world: the 'wine-red dress' is as fluid as Homer's wine-dark sea, the biscuit-eating is Bacchanalian in its excess, the 'street art you scraped off a wall on the way home' could be equally at home in inner-city Wellington or the streets of ancient Rome or Pompeii.

Jardine is an attentive reader not only of literary texts but of the everyday, alert to the odd details that bring a scene to life, finding exactly the right adjectives for the slipshod yachts, sturdy hens, decrepit dogs, scoffing (metaphorical) piglets. Her selection of poems turns over a loamy mixture of memory and desire, teeming with slaters, millipedes and complicated feelings, gritty and delicious.

From Apia to Parnell, Aro Park to the internet, ancient Rome to dreams of Venus, the poems in *AUP New Poets 7* take you places including the darkest reaches of emotional geographies lit up in startling new ways. Each poet writes with a rich vocabulary and distinct sense of rhythm, as they bring you bipedal goat-men, indestructible pumpkins, fat-soluble poisons, jellyfish, seagulls, eight-*tala* jugs of cocktails, loom weights, unseasonable journeys, deep-fried bananas, pet rabbits, destructive chickens, scars and tattoos, parataxis and ellipses, instructions on how to make toast, and more, so much more.

*Anna Jackson*

# Rhys Feeney

## soy boy

## the world is at least fifty percent terrible

waking up from a dream abt owning a house
for a moment i think i'm in utopia
    or maybe australia
        but then i see the little patches of mould on the ceiling
i roll over to check my phone
    but i forgot to put it on charge last night bc i was too tired
        why am i so fucking tired all the time
i should find some better alternative to sugar
i should find some better alternative to lying there in the morning thinking
Artificial Intelligence is a Fundamental Risk to Human Civilisation
    or what am i going to have for breakfast
        how can i reduce my environmental footprint
            but increase the impact of my handshake
i could try to eliminate the remaining dairy in my diet
o the money for quinoa besides
    cave people would have been fat if they'd had mountain dew
what is the alternative is there even an alternative
    what can i do what can anyone do
be a good patriot & eat a kilo of cheese with weet-bix
    drink soymilk from a deforested plantation in brazil
        or cowmilk from a waikato farm that runs right into the river
            while the CEO of fonterra gets a salary of $1.95 million
put a chicken in the oven
    where they have the most space they've had in their entire life
get on the bus go to work
    thank the driver think they look tired
check the apps everyone checks
    learn soon plastic in the ocean will outweigh the fish
sell clothes made in a sweatshop
    help a machine replace your job
say i don't like it but That's Just the Way It Is
    cry in the bathroom
ignore your co-worker eating caged eggs in the staffroom
    say how's the wife how's the kids
        don't think abt it don't

after work get drunk go to maccas don't eat anything
    walk out into the cold look up at the sky
ask where are the stars where is the moon
    why don't they come out
did we do something wrong did we

**overshoot**

1) start a bullet journal
each month count all the things
    you didn't have the resources for
        plan to do them again
2) food that made you feel full doesn't anymore
    you have little interest in things you normally enjoy
every time you go outside
        the air seems thicker        3) track the build-up
you had tomatoes in pots outside
        you threw them out
        the soil fell away like dust
4) everything you plant dies
        the leaves curl        the stems bend
you are spending more money on food
    track the build up
you know what is happening
    you are reaching your carrying capacity
scratch things from the list on the fridge
    5) give yourself time to yourself
light fresh linen candles
    & cry in the bath
        call it self-care
6) eat a whole loaf of bread in the dark
7) start working again
        the topsoil of your tolerance is gone
you break in two days
    this is called a feedback loop
your coping strategies don't work
        in this new atmosphere        8)
focus on eating a biscuit very slowly
    become distant from the ones close to you
        you can't make love during an extinction event
9) every time you breathe you are adding
    to a problem you can't understand
each day you wake up something
        has gone extinct while you slept

## how to make toast

    first       domesticate wheat      almost by accident
        realise you can survive like this     develop roots
stop living day by day     then      start to overproduce
      store cash crops     trade for necessities     trade for luxuries
look at you         you've gone & created capitalism
    now     form communities     nations
fight      make up     fight with better weapons     be jealous
    of your neighbour's wheat store     fit your mouth around language
say: toast     from *torrere*     *to burn*     hide your violent urges
    fight     toast to your health     neglect yourself
bake bread        let it go bad        cook it again
    repeat     figure out electricity without understanding electrons
design     a two-slot toaster     go to the supermarket
    buy bread     without understanding how it's made
put the bread in the toaster     cook it     forget about it
    put it in again     burn it     repeat     so much wheat
so many neighbours     think:     how did we get here
    put bread in the toaster     burn the forests     forget about it
genetically modify wheat     put it in again     fit your mouth
    around language
        burn it
            forget about it
    repeat

## (re)wilding

watching rewilding videos
    without leaving the house
eagles taking flight
    unsteady & uncertain
beagles learning how to play
sheep saved from the slaughter
    all fat & dehydrated
how it must feel
    enjoying the sunlight
        outside the hospital
            blinking in concrete glare
amazing to watch animals
    learning how to be animals
amazing to think we can
    put it all back
        ~~& pretend it never happened~~
watching rewilding videos
    that are attempts at atonement
watching ~~rewilding~~ videos
    thinking about the time
        they were applicable to you
trying to bridge ~~a metaphor between~~
    two ~~unique~~ helplessnesses
surviving ~~in the wild~~
    when you've never been in the wild
trying ~~to survive in~~ the wild
    ~~when the wild~~ is dying
~~surviving in the house~~
    ~~when the animal is~~ dying

# bioremediation

Dichlorodiphenyltrichloroethane, commonly known as DDT, has a normative half-life of two to fifteen years. This means it can take fifteen years for 50% of the chemical to break down.

    by friday      i am 50% used up      tho i'm tired      i make my weekly pilgrimage      taking foodscraps up to the compost bins at the innermost gardens

DDT was banned in Aotearoa in 1989. Twenty-one years after it was first banned by Hungary; twenty-seven years after the publication of *Silent Spring*.

    as you walk up majoribanks st      the congress of sparrows makes way for tūī song      sweeping across the evening soundscape

Thirty years later, 25% of the DDT used in 1989 can still be detected in the soil.

    the winding path past the entrance is dotted with marigolds to welcome bees      large parts of the gardens are being restored week by week

DDT is colourless, tasteless and mostly odourless.

    you stand in the gardens      & know it is coming to terms with the cruelty      the topsoil puts on brave face

When DDT breaks down it forms Dichlorodiphenyldichloroethylene (DDE) and Dichlorodiphenyldichloroethane (DDD).

    at the innermost gardens      community gardeners are trying to salvage the damp earth      they are planting mushrooms to cleanse Papatūānuku      they are making a web of healing fungi to extract pollutants      the gardeners sweat into the soil      the planter boxes are providing sustenance      pūhā      pikopiko      horopito

While DDD is classed a probable human carcinogen, the main issue is DDE.

> i can breathe in the gardens in a way i can't in the city     the air rich
>     full of love & nutrients

DDE is fat-soluble so it builds up in animal tissue. In this way it is like the lead in lead petrol and the fallout from atomic bombs. Unlike other poisons (e.g. 1080) which break down quickly, the only time DDE is removed from the body is when it is passed to the animal's young via breast milk.

> the burdens of inheritance are great     in the past 13 years
> i have accumulated a necklace from my grandmother     & half the
> world's plastic production

DDE and DDT are stored in body fat, and when one animal eats another the substance is transferred. This results in what is termed 'biomagnification', meaning each level of the food chain accumulates more of the substance.

> i am constantly reassured we are at the top of the food-chain
> in fact     there are two kfcs within walking distance of me
>     today i saw row after row of cars run over the carcass of a
> tarāpuka     which is to say magnification     i.e. the closer you look
> the worse it gets

Biomagnification threatens predators most, especially apex predators like native birds.

> mycoremediation is a process that uses fungi to decontaminate the soil
>     it is a process of healing     it requires patience & care
>     it requires sacrifice     the linking of whenua to hauora

In 1948, Paul Hermann Müller was awarded the Nobel Prize in Physiology or Medicine for discovering the insecticide properties of DDT.

    the mechanisms of degradation are not always clear     but the results
    seem to make themselves apparent     every billionaire's wikipedia
    page says philanthropist     the culprits of degradation have their
    own private gardens     when you run your hands through the soil
    you see nothing     when i wake i taste metal in my mouth

Many fungi are hyperaccumulators. They soak up the toxins and can later be removed from the soil.

    how much am i driven by urges     to help others at my own
    detriment

Rachel Carson's *Silent Spring* led to the formation in the USA of the Environmental Protection Agency.

    you must believe in hope     in the form of spring daffodils
        springing up when you have nothing left

There are ongoing efforts throughout Aotearoa to deal with DDT contamination, though more and more pesticides are entering awa, roto, moana and groundwater through agricultural runoff.

    i place my feet in the gardens     the soil doesn't know whether to
    accept me     i whisper to the earth     *how can we regain trust*

In 2016, 60% of Aotearoa's monitored rivers were unsafe to swim in.

        we breathe
            the earth hurts        as it remembers
                                    we breathe
            the whenua aches

## the president of the united states of america is crazy

'Is Mr. Trump Nuts?' / *Trump is Fucking Crazy* / *Trump is Nuts! An Illustrated Guide and Coloring Book to the Many Ways That Trump Has Gone Nuts* / 'Does Trump Suffer from Narcissistic Personality Disorder' / 'Here's a List of People Close to Trump Who May Think He's Seriously Nuts' / 'The President is Mentally Unwell – and Everyone Around Him Knows It' / *The Dangerous Case of Donald Trump: 27 Psychiatrists and Mental Health Experts Assess a President*

are some recent publications by various liberal institutions
are some examples of a small violence
a crack in an otherwise
                    welcoming brochure smile      saying:
The President Has a Personality Disorder
                              you're not like him you're not
~crazy~ like that     you are
not    Trump is    Mentally Unstable

    we don't judge for that one time when the state decided you were a risk
    to your own safety & the safety of others, so you were deemed unfit to
    be in public & institutionalised under the Mental Health (Compulsory
    Assessment and Treatment) Act 1992

when we say *psycho* we don't mean *psychotic*
                  (but at times the words are interchangeable)
we mean *psychopathic*     as in *Criminal Minds*     as in *sociopathic*
a term used in DSM-1 & associated with homosexuality & alcoholism

when we say come over Monday & we'll cook for you & it'll do you good
we mean wear long-sleeves so that we don't have to see It
the forest of red veins     spreading
like in *War of the Worlds*     the red weed
areoforming the Earth     turning the world into something
you can't bear to look at     A Crazy Person
with a Nuclear Button     a man obsessed with a
borderline     building a box around himself

putting bars                              on the windows of the hospital
eating                                    with only a plastic spoon
eating McDonalds in bed while crying because he had a hard day

    when we say: '[t]hose with borderline personality disorder are notorious
      for operating on the premise that feelings create facts'    (*USA Today*)
we are saying we believe in an objectivity
cut out of the earth by a surgeon     cut from a woman in stirrups
removed headfirst & still from the world        a New Atlantis
of scientific purity     a white world          a state of sanity

any deviation from the mean        a mutated gene
in a society that says it believes you
okay        of course we believe you        tell me about your mother
is there a history of mental illness in your family     how long has this been
    going on

## t/w: dsh

Sometimes someone I've known for a long time notices it. It makes me want to break myself down into individual morphemes, into quarks, to dissolve.

When they say *what happened?* they want a story. Which presents a problem: how do you narrativise it? You can't narrate a body without disembodying it.

Statistically, male rates of suicide are higher than female; however, women are more likely to engage in deliberate self-harm. This suggests these are different urges.

It is not hard for me to recount the details. But detail confuses people; they don't expect you to be able to talk about it. They don't expect you to point to your body as a system of signs.

My body as a system of chemical functions no longer functions the way it is supposed to. The amount of chemicals I put in my body that night has done something to the delicate balance of my immune system.

If they are different urges, then DSH can be best linked to the body. A desire to make emotional pain physical, to express hatred at your body, to self-punish.

Physical therefore real. Therefore, a symbol. Therefore, readable.

Occasionally, people ask me why I started to write poetry. My writing is connected to the chemicals in my body. The chemicals in my body are influenced by things I don't understand.

At school, I listen to students talk about themes from texts. How they relate to their experiences. I am a bad role model: I cannot understand how art & the things that happen to me connect.

I read Janet Frame & it is nothing like what happened to me. I have four drafts of stories based on my time in the psychiatric ward. I cannot understand the climate crisis, even though I think a lot about the cascading effects the climate crisis will have on the world.

I do not pretend to understand the science; I try to understand the story. I like the idea that there is a framework underneath all of this, even if it is created from language.

It is hard to tell how many people in Aotearoa harm themselves deliberately. The Ministry of Health only tracks hospitalisations from DSH.

In class, we look at *The Matrix*, where Morpheus quotes Baudrillard & calls the Wasteland *the desert of the real*. We discuss: *what is real?* The conclusion is reached that even if we think we are living in a simulation, we must go on day by day denying it.

I teach by drawing out links. If a character does this, *can* we make this conclusion about them? If a poem says this, *could* we link it to our own life? These questions rely on modal verbs that imply ability, permission, possibility.

I have no issues telling people on the internet the worst bits about myself.

Sometimes, in class, a student will ask me about my arm. I never tell them the truth, even though I think young people in Aotearoa need solid examples of mental health survivors.

I have no issue putting my diagnosis in a poem. The diagnosis that is hidden from my immediate medical record for fear of prejudgement. I am used to hiding important things from important people in my life. The Light Armoured Vehicle is not the only reason I didn't attend the parade.

I like the idea of cause & effect. The air gets hotter; there are more fires. More trees burn; more carbon is released. The air gets hotter; there are more fires.

DSH is prevalent in young people: around 18% of self-identified males & 29% of females surveyed in the Mental Health Foundation's Youth'12 survey had attempted it in some form.

I think when people notice for the first time, it changes something fundamental about how they perceive me. Something shifts in the network of interactions. The relative positioning of our bodies changes.

Moreover, 35% of same-sex- & 56% of both-sex-attracted young people had attempted it recently.

There is more to this than facts, more than details. Tim O'Brien calls this 'story truth'. We process our reality in narrative. Therefore, choices must be made; links must be formed.

Getting a tattoo is a choice; it is a way of claiming part of your body back from your genetics. You are asserting yourself over a system of body conception in our society.

In a way, scars are the same thing. They are not history but action. My scars are old but have yet to settle into soft hidden scar tissue. They are yet to cease hurting. When people ask about scars, they are asking about history, but it is an answer you can only give in present tense.

When you ask about a tattoo you don't say *when/how did you get that?* You ask what it means. You ask for the link between that symbol & the person.

I have no way to explain myself but in the positioning of events. At school I call this parataxis; at home I call this coping.

# roy g. biv

what happened is best explained through colour. not the black & white of stars seen from the city, rather the stabbing pain of long deep-red curtains when behind them there is the sound of something coming closer. no not that, something in between the two. how to explain the way the moonlight turned over & grew cold & there was nothing but grey grey only grey in the early morning apartment? how to explain that it has hollow bones yet still it is heavy? so hollow & so heavy that the flowers don't know where to look & still the moon is the only light & you can romanticise it & you can see beauty in it but the wildlife can't survive. that is the cold truth. it turns your fingers black & it burns behind your eyes. you fight. you resist. you become the deepest dwelling bacteria, hiding inside a rock made of dirty dishes until at last you can't bear it anymore. it is all too much. it is all too much to bear. you can't cope & the colours now are returning home from a trip abroad, they are brighter & harsher & it hurts to look, it hurts to imagine. the red is everywhere & the grey is now steel blue, a coping mechanism, & there are some weeds growing flowers but they aren't any one colour; they are fluctuating, they are part of a dichotomy, a sine curve you'll come to hate because the stars have colour if you look long enough & it is beautiful & it is horrible & what are you meant to do with all these shades? breathe. the sky is sky blue again; what it means is anyone's guess. a colour chart could help but it's always twisting, contorting, a sunset cityscape beautiful one moment & the spitting image of dread the next. trying to understand yourself by talking it out & testing, shading in the circles around your eyes. you can use the word *saffron* or *crimson* or *velvet* or *scarlet*, but you are talking about bleeding, bleeding dry, dried up. it's impossible to get a straight answer from yourself. the screaming is always there just sometimes it takes on a different form, sometimes it wants to dance & sometimes it wants to creep slightly closer to the edge & sometimes, sometimes, you'll want to do something, you'll want to do something very bad indeed & you'll think about it always & one day & one day & one day

# MCMI-III

*(with lines from the Millon Clinical Multiaxial Inventory, third edition)*

i dream every morning on the way to work. i dream of road-cone orange flowers lining both sides of a long path. the sun through the bushes feels like a thermonuclear explosion in the permafrost. there must be beauty in there somewhere, but i can't bear to look. i dream of game shows & the million-dollar final question. really, i dream everything: tins of tomatoes & tins of coconut milk & the price of the bus & the price of housing & the price of living & the price of not dying. i dream of shedding my skin like a polyester jumper sheds in the wash. i'm too embarrassed to admit my problems as frankly as i should. i dream about long clouds composed entirely of silver linings like planets stripped of their crust. i dream about a morning with a firm handshake. i dream about a world where people love the flowers next to the motorway. i pick flowers & crush them in my fingers. they don't even smell of diesel fumes. i only see it fall, fall apart. nothing good comes of it. lately i've been feeling blue lately i've been feeling down & out. i flew over the atlantic thirty times last year. i have not seen a car in the last ten years. lately i dream of long red curtains & black & white tiles. an utterly other place where we can be our best selves or at least other selves or at least somewhere we can forget our worst selves like a small- to medium-size family-owned getaway home with a complimentary breakfast hamper. i dream of a red sun that hangs low & never sets but somehow this horizon is beautiful. it looks you right in the eye & says it doesn't think of itself as a problem. i'm considered a tough and unsentimental person. i dream of reading up against a damp wall, of the mould that grows under my fingernails under the chest of drawers under the sun. i think i am making my life look worse than it really is by my responses here. i dream of the rain on the roof which sounds like a pot boiling over. i dream of dirty dishes & there's a weather warning out so i lay them all outside on the patio to let the rain fill them up. it doesn't clean them properly. how could it? they've sat by the sink for a week now. still, they look all the better for it.

**mariner_1.txt**

you are trying / to shoot for venus / you are missing some part of the equation / somewhere there are two things / that should not / be together / a sentence ends prematurely / a discontinuation loop / getting out of control / you are / dreaming of a whirlwind / a runaway / greenhouse / you are trying / running away / to shoot for venus / six seconds before / separation / it is getting very warm / in your dreams / it is all spinning / unauthorised pitch-yaw manoeuvre / dreams of venus / resemble the pacific / the pressure / the heat / the kernel error

## brutalism

standing in the carpark of the psychiatric ward / looking at
the anaemic architecture of concrete & corrugated iron /

monolithic shapes under the overcast sky / a 1960s dream
of the future reclaimed by vines & rust / it's obvious that

the things we do in the name of rebuilding / are not always
future-proof / i have said such horrible horrible things /

they remain / like the invariable leaden background in your
photographs / i have the urge to embrace this aesthetic even

when i know that / concrete is the most destructive material
that humans have ever created / that every year we pour

enough concrete to / cover every maunga and fill in every
awa in the north island / that after water it is the most used

substance in the world / that concrete will soon outweigh
the biomass of every living thing / how much of what i

enjoy stems from coping mechanisms / formed out of
necessity when faced with a disabling system / now i find

peace in waiting rooms & windowless offices / with
sedative manila walls & the unlocatable breathing of a/c /

surveying the hospital campus i find nothing but beauty / in
the same way i wake up strangely reassured after a dream

where i'm buried alive / dirt shoved into my smiling mouth

## pripyat on a good day

there are men in the red woods
who do outrageous things
& live to tell abt it
what i mean is there are
boys in the red woods combing the
fallout from the hair of wild foxes
there are boys who are object shelters
themselves who are holding on to
deposited uranium who smile
with glowing teeth
there are boys climbing in & out
of sarcophaguses out & in
of confinement structures
& out & out of exclusion zones
what i really mean is there are boys
who are coming out
of the red woods who are
shovelling the dirt over the radioactive
pines who are doing what even
lunokhod couldn't do i mean
they are enduring wildfires
in a place where the groundwater can kill u
& sometimes shovelling dirt
is harder than driving around on the moon
sometimes between the reactor-room doors
& the fence marking the borderline
it gets a little confusing
there are lines everywhere
running right under our feet
all i am trying to say is that sometimes
u cross the line in the middle of the night
& there is no one around to see it

**current mood**
*after Pip Adam*

there's a feeling in your chest
& it's not going anywhere
it has the permanence
of a pile of used plastic
floating around
on the oil-slick surface
but worse is the realisation that
beneath that there's probably a growing
colony of single-use coping strategies
the thought of it makes your heart
beat like a battery broiler
you have so much inside you
you've spent your whole life in a
cage with no room to turn around
the cheapest way to calm it all down
is to cut the lights     listen
to the heaving of all the people
shoulder to shoulder     listen
the feeling that you were wrong
won't go away / you thought you
were a god / but this sushi container
will outlive you / this phone battery is stuck in your throat /
every breath is more $CO_2$ / from here / there is no way out / it is piling
up / you are standing / on an island / made of styrofoam / you are screaming /
in the pit / of your stomach / you are swimming / in the ocean / & it's everywhere

## the great pumpkin war

standing in the kitchen crying
        beaten by a vegetable
thought by now it would be easier
people have suggested this (people i trust)
        the myth of progress
you do something every day it gets easier
in reality each day the dirt accrues
        it multiplies between cupboard doors
i am running out of resources
i am getting further & further into
        the ten-year warranty on the fridge compressor
one day soon i will have to pick up the knife
        & address the pumpkin in the room
bought so cheaply from the farmers' market
        now growing larger by the day
taking up all the bench space
        i fear for the fruit bowl
my mother says to drop it from a height
        she throws hers down the stone garden steps
my previous attempt resulted in
        twenty minutes lost to searching for an unscathed pumpkin
trying to break open a pumpkin at night
        is like starting a winter war in russia
i am letting everything get out of control
        i sleep knowing it is getting worse
i do not think i can win at this
        i do not think i can carry on in any capacity

## improvise / adapt / overcome

see a burst water main
    thirst for the clear water
like a cat rejecting a $100 pet fountain
    in favour of gutter water

tell yourself it is the animal in u
    rejecting the excessive corporatisation
        of the public space
rejecting the electric scooters
    scattered as if mid-rapture

tell urself it is the animal in u
    craving something it has never had
        a clean body of water to link itself
like a veal calf licking the bars of its cage
    to get some iron into its diet

remember bear grylls drinks his own piss
it's ok bc people want to watch it
caged veal calves drink their own piss
it's ok bc no one can see it

ur whiskers touch the sides of the bowl
    triggering a survival instinct
u will need this during the water riots

why does no one else you see care that there has
    been water running free down the road
        for days & days & days?

## pull down firmly to start the flow of oxygen

whenever i fly i lose all respect for urban planners
      i've never seen a city that looks aesthetic from the sky
i guess we have that in common
not organised enough to be successful
      not spontaneous enough to be enjoyable
ah     i can see my house from here
it looks very fragile     so close to the harbour
      a tiny concrete box     but not in a cute soviet way
all the houses have different personalities
      & the ones next to mine are all cunts
who laugh evilly in italian suits     while eating
cigar-infused māui dolphin cocktails
i am sorry again for getting angry  i am just
      trying to find new ways to breathe
as the city spills over land
      i know what ur going to say
          it is hypocritical to fly
if it makes u feel better
when the plane hits some rough air
      it makes my stomach
          jump through little gold hoops
when it does this i think i am abt
      to have a panic attack
my brain so coded now to this
      ~chemical fuckery~
i have to remember my body
      has more than two emotions
there is a whole city in my sight
      i could walk from one end
to the other     i can go home
      any time i like     i am flying
very high in the sky     a marvel really

## to be stable

let me tell you a story:      in theoretical physics
                    quantum chromodynamics
describes the action of the strong force     which holds together
       the smallest layers of existence      where the building blocks of
                 nuclei       (hadrons)      exist
       to be stable                 a hadron must have no net force
at the sub-hadron layer     electrical charge is no longer applicable
       instead     we find ourselves in a world
of      *spin*      *flavour*      *colour*      life seems so strange
             words jump out at me          from dim corners
yesterday i stood in front of a class         all wearing VR headsets
       we looked at a lake in Russia           from space
how to assimilate this knowledge          when the forces that
       dictate our lives are not always clear
the Pauli exclusion principle suggests              particles with
       ½ spin      cannot occupy the same quantum state
like most things that are impossible     there is an example of this
       to resolve this paradox             scientists turned to
analogy:     light         colour is the arbitrary name
       for one state of a subatomic particle
a hadron      such as a neutron       consists
       of three (3) quarks      which are each assigned
a colour:      red (R)         green (G)         or         blue (B)
       after the core visible spectrum             to be stable
a hadron must have no net colour          like sunlight
       through the morning window      a hadron
must hold itself together in its ordinariness
       it must tell itself a story about          progress
even though it knows that analogous links form
       the base of storytelling
you can pull quarks apart in collisions        you can pull words apart
       until there is no meaning left     just unstable graphemes
when you pull at your skin hard enough        it leaves
       red marks         blue bruises             to be stable
you can think of your moods as colours        but      i think

      we are always explaining one thing with another
              while the world goes on burning
never getting to the core of it
    like peeling an onion    until there is nothing left
which is one analogy    that still works
    even when you pull away all the colour
trust me    i'd rather believe the world were an artichoke
    but i've never seen one    not even in the supermarket

# Ria Masae

# What She Sees from Atop the Mauga

## Native Rivalry

Saipipi, Savai'i, Samoa

Nana Se'ela asked me once
*'E ke mana'o e fai sau malu?'*
i turned to her, my *makas* widening in shock
i gazed down at the jellyfish, seagulls and crosses
under the stars
tattooed around her thighs
in my Samoglish i questioned
'me? *Ae ā* Mum?'
Nana's throat made a raspy sound
like she was going to spit on the sand

true – Mum was lost to *Niu Sila* burdens
disguised as *pālagi* exoticness
had less time for village matters
she was spread between two motherlands now
the first, native to her tongue
rooted from the sands and plantations
where her mother gave birth to her
the second, native to her offspring
where she became a mother herself.
Mum was *fa'a pālagi*, out of necessity
i was *pālagified* by consequence
so, was I much different?

i tilted my face up to the stars
that were more familiar to me
than the ones on Samoan thighs.
without turning to her, i answered
*'Leai fa'afetai*, Nana.'
i felt her stare at me for a long pause
before puffing on her rolled tobacco.
we sat there silently looking at the night sky
until we were tired and went to sleep
side by side on a *falalili'i* in her *fale*.

**Apia, Upolu, Samoa**

I sit on the rocks along the sea wall in Apia
and squint across the night shaded water
at Upolu's sister island, Savai'i.
Behind me *Amelika* and rasta jams blast from nightclub speakers
*ie faitaga*-wearing policemen stroll up and down
taking occasional puffs of *mea lele* / make-you-fly smoke
from the snaky trail of *cheeehooo!* drunks.
A woman hoarses laughter that makes
the *fetu* tattoos on her breasts jiggle.
A man breathes Valima proposals
to a girl who is not his wife.
My eyes are bleary from eight-*tala* jugs
of cocktails with names that sound like
the devil's temptations to Savai'ian ears.
I wonder if Savai'i looks at us
under the same stars
and hears our debauchery noise
across the same waters
and is thankful that the sea separates
our fall from grace
from Her *Pa'ia* Spirit?

## Vinyl Sundays A-Track

We genuflect.
Men dressed by their wives in their Sunday best
kneel on planks of uncross.
Women pass over bread to their children
to deposit in pass-around plates
for confessional clean slate.

Samoan choir sing praises to Jewish mythology.
Tagaloa spits an eye for an eye at our irreverence.
He laughs, foreseeing
my first taste of alcoholic lust
is sipping the blood of *Keriso*.

## Intersection

She sits at her window
staring down at the city lights.
Her scared, her scarred, her marred wrists
hugging her carpet-burnt knees.
The waves in her hair
no longer carry the scent of her Pacific Ocean
but burn with the stink of
roll-your-own cigarettes.
Nylon lashes from a discounted pack of ten
shroud her deadened eyes;
deadness disguised as apple promises
from 'God, why have you forsaken me?' corners
on Beat Street.

He shuffles towards the aluminium bin
searching for sustenance to feed
his dazed, his glazed, his blazed eyes.
Tangled threads of purpose and aspirations
fray from the hem of his flea-ridden coat
                         / blanket
                         / shelter
                         / all.
His City Mission donated boots
crush amber crystals
from shattered red Lions and liquid Tuis.
It's munch time, crunch time
get in fucking line time
on Beat Street.

Her thoughts drift to her village life
a dirt road lined with fruiting trees
that led to the river where women washed their bodies
and refreshed their souls.
Now she lives in the city
where the streets rape her pocket full of dreams

and leave her bleeding, pleading
for a bag of artificial bliss.
Shame in the game! Ashamed of her name
on Beat Street.

She sees him and sits a little straighter.
He cradles the brown paper package
out of the rubbish and gently unfolds the opening
with dirt-filled fingernails
and grins. He pivots, looks up,
she's sitting inside the frame of the window
a small smile on her painted lips,
and like every other night
he calls out,

'My queen, Mona Lina!
Lina of the *masina*,
the beat beat beat of my heart.
*Fa'afetai*.'

Her smile broadens
as he flourishes a page's bow then ambles away.
She has never replied to his outbursts
and he has never sought a reply from her
he is joyful enough for her offerings
she is grateful for his words.
Grateful, hopeful, thankful
that her existence
is the beat-beat-beat
of *someone's* heart
on Beat Street.

## docket dates

```
*  The waitress                       pops
                      flesh bubble gum              from her
                      doll blow up lips
+  Salmon tongue uniform              slicks over
                      chest and rear                mounds
+  Discoloured apron   –    impotent   –
                      does not conceal              stains
+  She comes                           swaying
                      stands erect                  before me
                                        cocks
                      her hip                 to one side
+  Feather lashes                      raise       to showcase
                      four-poster bed / back car seat
                                        eyes
+  Top buttons                         unfastened   flashing
                      freckles                     above lilac lace
                                        covered breasts
+  Passion gloss nails  pull                       a pointy pencil
                      from behind   her
                                    thrice-pierced  ear
                      touches it to a              fake (it)
                      leather     flip (over)
                                                   notebook
                                                   and waits
+  What's the special  of the day,   doll?
                      throaty utterance:
+  Deep               fried banana   on sliced      peaches

                                                   _____
                                                   *with cream*
                                                   _____
```

34

## *Mā*

You look at me plastic
    'Why don't you have a *malu*?'

    Pfft:
the memories of my ancestors
and stories of their villages
are not tattooed on my skin
because I am no kin
to *pālagi* parlour needles
nor do I feel I have earned the tap-tap-tap
of the *sausau* mallet on the *au*
– the fine-tooth comb of bone –
held in the sacred *lima* of a *tufuga*.

I have no desire for my body
to advertise *pepelo*
to billboard *bullkaka*
to grandstand airs
for show
for fashion
for Likes.
I have no need for my *tino*
to house my *mana*
in a sham temple
like you.

## Vinyl Sundays B-Side

After church
men smoke rollies in the carpark
their backs to the 'No Smoking' sign.
Women with backstabbing eyes
smile neon lipsticks
as if painted jujus can mask bullkaka.

I only sing at night because Lā envies me.
Once, it growled, *Suga, stop stepping on my dick!*
and tried to burn my voice.
My hymns now flicker
along Masina whispers.

## Weekend Idol

She zips leather second skin over naïve bones
smears luscious across her chapped lips
pulls fuck-me-but-don't-fuck-me purple boots
pass her knobby knees
and styles her hair in front of the mirror
without once looking into her reflected eyes.

Her 1986 Mitsubishi Chariot
smokes through over-the-bridge traffic
then swerves onto Park-and-Pray Street.
She strides through neon pillars of archaic pursuits
and strips her nakedness down to her mask.
Licking eyes and sniffing tongues
bid thrills that pay her bills.
To dance to this music
she musics to the dance
of Sunday solar systems.

## Black Days

She peeks through the window for the first time in –
she can't remember how many days it's been.
Her net curtain needs a wash but that won't happen until –
well, whenever it passes.
The children next door prance feverishly on the cooked pavement.
Sprinkles of gravel indent the spongy soles of their primary school feet
like hundreds and thousands pressed into buttered slices of soft bread.
Pastel colours chalk their bubblegum imaginations onto the driveway.
She sways on her feet, disorientated
looking through the portal of her shadowed window frame
into an otherworld of suns and laughter –
she hasn't opened her thermal curtains in a while.
Her letterbox has spewed store catalogues onto the grass –
too much junk isn't good for anyone or anything.
The birthday balloons tied to the letterbox next door
bob like buoys in a quiet ocean –
waver like breaths in a dark house.

## Chipped China

How can Brian –
the street bully –
be this delicate giant?

Eleven-year-old Tūmema
peered through the slits
of the wooden slats
under Brian's house.

The same thick fingers
that had dragged her by the hair
across the school field

nimbly raised a china cup
to the porcelain doll's
love-heart lips.

## SkyCity Scraps

A nomad, a no-man
roams a concrete be-wilderness of steel trees with glass roots
that suckle over-population's sewage from synthetic udders.

A towering syringe built from seamless stones and black mirrors
injects the wishful with debt and depression and false build-ups
that plummet to real nothings.
        cash in your chips
        chip in your cash
        roll the dice
He psyched himself to roll with the punches
but idioms fool idiots and the punches knocked him to his knees
onto a cross of nails discarded by an ancient demi-god
who walked on water and swam through sand
– a semi-god who is not intended for him anyway
for he is not a man risen from the sea or sprouted from the land,
but a man fallen from the sky.
        This *ka-ching! ka-ching!* planet is as false as prophets
        who preach the apocalypse of our soul system
        to those who already lost their souls at the devil's scraps table.
Long past destruction, he bluffed he was still in cruise control.
Sure, sometimes adjusting the gears was necessary, yet
he was confident the tread of his prize-winning tyres
would grip the snaking road for a lifetime guarantee.
But Fortuna, who mockingly is the secret lover of Madness,
created a rollercoaster highway that wrote off the nomad's family chariot
        and now, abandoned
        he drags his bare feet
        along paths of gravel dreams.
This nomad believed it was just a sideline leisure
when it stopped being fun, he would merely dust off his middle-class jacket
and stroll through the green-light EXIT to greet the rising moon.
This no-man believed his compulsion was trivial
just as cancer sticks, devil's nectar and legal highs
were sanctioned in all-man's law.

Yet, as he shuffles past legions of
midnight men lost amongst afternoon ghosts
he realises Iustitia was blindfolded all along,
unable to see her justice scales balanced lawful corruptions
and their illegal counterparts as equal rulers of the nameless.
> This nomad, this no-man
> > has become one of the nameless.
> > He is but one rusted nail amongst thousands
> > on that discarded cross.

The setting sun colours the road ahead
a deep shade of sorrow.

# There is No Translation for Post-Natal Depression in the Samoan Language

- *E suga*, did you hear bout Susana? Susana say, da doctor say she godda bostal debress.
- *E ā?* Da doctor send her what in the bost?
- *Se* noooo. Da doctor say Susana godda *ma'i* call bostal debress.
- What? What's wrong wif Susana's breasts?

Growing up I had never heard of post-natal depression.
It was never smelt around smoking barbecues
where uncles sipped from sweaty beer bottles in the summer.
It was never heard amongst the clutter and laughter
of my aunties' kitchens on cousins' birthdays.
I never tasted it in the raw fish, *sapasui* and *kalo* lathered in coconut cream
that blessed the trestle tables at *aiga* feasts.
As for depression, well
we've all mourned a loss –
had a shit day –
experienced misfortune of sorts.
All commonplace and natural
all temporary.

- *Se* no! Bostal debress not sumfing wrong wif her *susu*. Susana's doctor say it make her grazy after Tupu was born.
- How? Tupu just a *pepe*. Dat stupid *pālagi* doctor, he da one who grazy.
- Susana said it make her cry and get *ika* all da time.
- *E*, tell Susana she bedda stop being *makagaga*. Tupu the *pepe*, not her!

I was always the independent one
the 'strong' one
So I clenched my smile to hide my diet of
silent rage breakfast
black-dog-tired lunch
salt-wet pillows dinner
and snacks of autopilot
to keep the carnivore in my head

from gnawing at my sanity and self-worth.
All these secrets I hid in the cracks of my mirror
until the inner voice of daggers and stones
smashed it and threatened to adorn me
with a necklace of shards threaded with my veins.

Against all expectations of a strong woman
of *fa'a Samoa* upbringing
of socially accepted everyday conversation
I finally picked up the phone and rang you.
Through my gagging sobs all I could manage to croak was
'I think I'm having a breakdown.'
I heard the impatience and annoyance in your voice
scolding about something irrelevant and superficial
before you hung up.
You didn't *hear* me.

- I never heard of a bostal debress. No such fing in Samoa.
- I bet it's *pepelo*. Somefing *pālagis* just make up becos dey lazy.
- *la gā*. Just an excuse not to clean da house and look after da gids.
- *E*, Susana *fia pālagi* now with her new boyfriend, and pretend she godda *pālagi ma'i*.
- Poor Tupu, poor *pepe*. Useless, lazy parents.

A cousin came to visit.
We spoke in awe of our aunties in the motherland
how they would go into hospital in the morning
pop out a new cousin
then be back home that same evening
to multiple outstretched brown hands
welcoming the newborn into the extended *alofa*.
In Samoa, a village really does raise a child.
Depression does not thrive in communities
where isolation and individualism are alien concepts.
My cousin and I joked

how we should've had our babies in the motherland
so that by the time our offspring came back into our own hands
they'd be old enough to get jobs and support us.

So, I understand your reaction
to that distant ago phone call now
and after so long
I forgive you.

## Satellite

A crucifix of tubular lights

carried up Mount Roskill by orange vest workers;

Auckland Council Christianity

burns noughts and crosses confessions.

## Parousia

Jesus died this morning

in a nameless alleyway
hunched between an
ex-jailbird and a homeless girl.

I saw him last night
> *tickling the feet of fa'afafine*
> *with his bearded kisses.*

I heard him last night
> *laughing with hardened Magdalenas*
> *over plastic cups of street brew.*

I felt him last night
> *kiss cleansing across the depression*
> *furrowed on my forehead.*


You missed him –
the Second Coming has come and gone.

You were too preoccupied
scouring penthouse suites in trump hotels
> *singing psalms to abusers on podiums*
tasting bleach from make-it-rain teeth
> *and stroking feathers of corrupt wings.*

Did you not learn from his first visitation
that he would come as One
of the wandering and uncrowned?

Did you not learn from his first stopover
that sinner and saviour
walk shoeless side by side
along bleeding crossroads?


Jesus died this morning

in a nameless alleyway
beneath your feet
while your nose pointed to the skies.

## Jack Didn't Build Here

This is the house that Dad built.
Foundation laid with stories,
from sitting under the *ulu* tree
to learnings from *pālagi* scholarship:
for wife, for offspring, for *aiga*.
Sunday School teachings echo in his mother-tongue
dotted with Oxford Dictionary words.

This is the house that Lange built.
Southside Prime Minister. The only home
in the hood with a pool. He invited the locals
– his Mangere locals – over to swim
and understood the pressures of *fa'alavelave*,
cos he brown on the inside like that.

This is the house that Mum built.
Chandelier hangs over the heads of relo
poker players, cheating and laughing on
the woven *fala*. Celebration trestle tables
laden with islands of *sapasui*, *oka*,
*fa'alifu talo*, *palusami* and *umu* pork
surrounding a pavlova cheesecake.

This is the house that Key built.
Double-glazed windows within a security-code gate.
His pool stretches across his Parnell palace
where renters are never invited to take a dip.
Instead he swims regular laps to drown the reality
of midnight figures huddled inside torn sleeping bags
outside glaring high-fashion mannequin stores.

This is the house I am building.
Born in brown central, raised in gentrified central,
now in State House central. Wallpaper designed with parents' language
smudged into Samoglish. One post carved from

the ancient *va'a* of bloodline ocean wayfinders.
Other post, a mighty kauri etched with Grimms' fairytales,
and Chinese script I feel for but can't yet translate.

What house will Jacinda build?
Will it accommodate the next generation?
Will it enable my daughters to build their own homes
of tangata whenua foundations and *fa'a Samoa* roofs
in this *pālagi*fied City of Sales?

## The Artistry Effect

The distinguished weaver
    proceeds
        with skill and care
           to weave
                a fine cloak
                    of communities – of life.
                    The artist
                        carving a tree
                            follows the grain
                            of timber,
                            works in harmony

                  with its natural character –
              these significant spells
          of kinship with all creatures
      seen as living on
in the carving or cloak.

We cannot simply
    govern the process
        of the artist –
           what criterion we might use for worthiness.
           We cannot choose
                what is going to reflect
                    someone's essence.

                    Look
                      once more
                          at the uses
                          we might make
                          of enhancing value.

                      What is of importance
                  is the idea,
                in the abstract –
              in the impossible.

## Maker

She dyes her hair fifty shades of God
perfumes her neck with Milky Way
laces her stomp-the-stadium sneakers
then hitches an electric thunder to her garden of creation
where Her Word *breathes* through Pioneer speakers –

>Let there be sound!

Genesis fingertips scratch life-beats on a vinyl universe
spinning galactic spheres on turntables

>Her A-track.

Comets pop candy from Her mouth
booming panoramic rhythm to underground applause.
Star-dusty feet *taptaptap* eternal BPM –

>oonst oonst oonst oonst

>>*Big Bang smoulder*
>>*smells of nothing*
>>*yet of everything*
>>*like water.*

## My Vā

*The Vā is a sacred space of in-betweens*
*– a relational space*
*that holds everything together in oneness.*

There is a *Vā* between my thighs.
A *pa'ia* space where
binaries such as *alofa* and pain,
and the passing of old and the coming of new
coexist in swirling tangles.
When I open my thighs
a V points its arrow tip to where
the aroma of earth, ocean and sky blend
and exist invisible but real.
It is a consecrated space born to me –
my space of liberty to use, exhibit and offer
in any way I see fit.
Or so I thought . . .

There is a *Vā* between my legs
where men have trespassed shamelessly.
They saw the V as a neon arrow
pointing to mere pussy.
Tricksters who invaded my *tapu* territory
with their ungodly feet, assaulting hands and stabbing semen.
Cowards who hissed their conquests
of hellish ecstasy while pillaging my Eden
until I dug my grave on my own *fanua* beneath them
to cocoon in the numbness of the Black forever.
Or so I thought . . .

There is a *Vā* between my feet.
A sanctified Creator place
where I am the image of God.
Where old souls nest to grow new blood, tissue and bone
before exploding from duet rhythm to solo drum

into this world.
This is where I am entrusted with my most holy duty
– that of Mother.
This is where I relearnt what love is.

Yes, there is a *Vā* between my thighs
where I've been ripped to trauma by men with no *mana*
but I willingly tore my universe to birth Big Bang daughters
who gave me reason to riot against black holes
that sucked the brilliance of my star.

Yes, there is a *Vā* between my feet
where I have bled the blasphemy of unwanted men
then flooded red tsunami for my offspring
who restored my faith in trust.

Yes, there is a *Vā* between my legs
where I have clawed through misery filth
to resurrect in the gift of newborn hope
to find the conviction to reclaim
the blessed hearth of my sacred space
granted to me and me alone
by my burning *agaga*.

# Prologue

They think her strange,
truth be told.
Identity – the concept
    *confuses her*
    *constricts her*
    *concludes her*
like 'The End' of a book
when the story has only begun:
    *in the beginning was hero unbreathing*
    *in the beginning was stagnant pulse*
    *in the beginning was chaos birthing*
    *in the middle were mouths unkissed*
    *in the middle was climatic ascent*
    *in the middle was falling*
    *then just like that –*
    *The End.*
The complexities of journey and resolution untold.


They preach she change her identity
she stares at I in the mirror
    thinking on        Identity
    and asks,          'I dent it, why?'
    They leer,         'Eye dem titty!'


Yes, they think her strange.
Truth be told,
she struggles with herself.
Sundays
    *she burns like a flame atop a candle*
    *illuminating remedies to her confusion*
    *(remedies that wear off too soon).*
Mondays to Thursdays
    *she shadows against walls*

>  *trying desperately to be the flame*
>  *but only dancing its silhouette.*

Fridays and Saturdays
>  *she is melting wax*
>  *transforming into something eccentric and unknown*
>  *– she doesn't take well to change.*

Then there are the days
>  *when The End comes suddenly,*
>  *erasing her story –*
>  *when she shudders alone in the dark*
>  *blown out by unseen lips.*

Claudia
Jardine

The
Temple
of Your
Girl

Three Excerpts from

# A Gift to Their Daughters
*A Poetic Essay on Loom Weights in Ancient Greece*

1. Introduction

'Textile manufacture' is the sound my mother makes when she tries to speak with a needle held between her lips.

Ancient Greek written sources share a common view of the female domestic role as one that occurred indoors, with the key concern being the effective organisation of the *oikos*.

*Oikos* means something like family.

Central to this domestic role was the processing of raw materials into usable forms, and so women are often depicted as closely associated with not only domestic work but also its tools.

My grandmother combs wool to knit clothes for her thirteen great-grandchildren. No one asks her to.

I should tell her about the pots that show women carding wool against their naked shins.

Scandalous and entirely impractical.

Recent scholarship on the loom weight makes a strong case for the close examination of material culture as a means to explore the interpersonal relationships of women, their domestic labour and the spaces they worked in (underrepresented, repetitive, determined by the season).

It does not take long before I find rooms filled with women working.

The haberdashery is busy.

My mother and I weave through the crowd to the tidy shelf with the needles.

I have a habit of pulling on loose threads.

2. The Importance of Textile Manufacture for the Relationships of Women

A loom weight is a small object made with the purpose of holding down the lengthwise threads on a vertical warp-weighted loom.

Clean the raw wool, comb it out and then spin it.

When I was little my brother tried to brush my hair. He did not use enough force. The brush got stuck.

Then, the loom was set up and the weaving began. On a black-figure *lekythos* by the Amasis Painter from the sixth century BCE, women are depicted carrying out these tasks together.

The loom is taller than they are.

I ask a colleague to hold his hands above his head for the duration of my presentation. He sweats.

One weaves, one stands ready with more thread.

Most of the ancient and prehistoric representations of wool-working show two or more women working together, suggesting that the practice was more efficient when completed in groups, and perhaps that it was more agreeable to work with a companion.

On another vase, Penelope sits at the loom, alone, hurriedly unpicking another day's work.

The weights clink to her in confusion. Is he dead, or not?

She cries because she does not know, but he would love this trick.

Weaving provided women with a means to socialise and help one another, strengthening their own emotional associations to the *oikos* and to textile manufacture itself.

The school hall is filled with Berninas, Singers, Vikings and Behringers.

Our mums are making cat-convict costumes for the school musical, a mash-up of plagiarised Lloyd Webber and local gossip.

I already hate *CATS – The Musical.*

### 3. The Importance of Textile Manufacture for Making Connections

Textile manufacture was also necessary for the induction of new women into the *oikos*.

I think about all the queens on *Drag Race* who do not know how to sew.

In Xenophon's *Oikonomikos*, Ischomachus reports to Socrates that his fourteen-year-old wife 'knew no more than how, when given wool, to turn out a cloak'.

Prior to the widely believed early age of marriage, a girl would probably not have been large enough or strong enough to work the loom.

The dread when one of my friends, at age eleven, announces to the group that she is going to lose her virginity when she is fourteen.

'But that's only three years away,' we say.

She reneges.

'Actually, fifteen.'

Ischomachus, acknowledging that his young bride is not as skilled in wool-working as she could be, nevertheless still encourages her to teach a maid how to spin, and thus 'to double her worth'. The teaching of textile manufacture, Xenophon suggests, was the responsibility of the manager of the *oikos*.

I drop out of my Year 7 knitting club because no one is paying attention to me.

A new bride was integrated into the *oikos* through working as part of the group and building relationships with other women by sharing in the domestic labour.

My dad is furious when I decide to take a textiles class in Year 10. My mother has a needle in her mouth during this conversation.

The skills learned and the textiles made were also by no means frivolous, as a column of the Gortyn Code states that on leaving her marital home after a divorce, a woman was entitled to take half of what she had woven while married.

Is there a moment in which a man finds a loom weight on the floor, in some sunny corner, and wonders what he has lost?

Am I romanticising ancient Cretan divorce?

The involvement of young girls in wool-working groups, therefore, enabled their induction into their bridal home, while also providing them with the means to maintain personal wealth, should they depart from it.

She teaches me how to cross-stitch. It takes all five seasons of *Breaking Bad* to complete the paternal family crest. A belt and a spur, *cave adsum*. I don't think to ask about hers.

# The Flower Crown of Sulpicia

**Sulpicia 3.13 – Etta James**

Love has come such Love such Love
more shame in stashing blushes
than being famous for getting naked

Venus delivered
put in my pocket
Love

Venus delivered
my telling joy
let those with no joy speak mine

I want no safe letter
not no one reading before Love might –
scandal! oh please

beaten by keeping face
let me say it let me bear it
worth meets worthy

Sulpicia 3.14 – Stevie Nicks

hateful natality
is here

*why was I even born?*

to be spent in abusive country
trite in its lack of Cerinthus

no saccharine city
no suitable villa for this girl
no! cold rivulet amongst the vines

Messalla
uncle ugh
always with this unseasonable journey

taken against my will
that will surrendered
that will you never suffer to be

## Sulpicia 3.15 – Katy Perry

have knowledge
the journey abolished
through your bitter girl's courage

now
might I
be your birthday present?

let us pass the day
in everything
that you did not imagine

to be coming to you

### Sulpicia 3.16 – Nina Simone

how nice it is
your surrender to apathy
me
in decay

let you have your harlots and their baskets
pinned down in a pile of their own togas

not this daughter of Servius

sting of the pessimists
fancy me giving in
to a nameless bed

## Sulpicia 3.17 – Madonna

surely surely
your piety extends to the temple of your girl
altars afire with fever?

why choose to conquer
wretched infection
you not wishing it too

what is the use in evisceration
if you can stomach it
heart unmoving?

## Sulpicia 3.18 – Julie Andrews

so hot
my light
these past few days

I mean
of all the stupid things I've done
I just

I left you alone last night
coveting my veiled
adoration

## Ode to Goon
*For Tom and Domino*

So there's me, sprawled across the bed
eating bits of biscuit like Bacchus,
and you, half out of a suit,
looking at me as if I'm street art
you scraped off a wall on the way home.
Wine-red dress spilt on the floor,
so drunk we pulled the mattress from the bed
and crushed a packet of biscuits.
And while you pondered how it was
that I had come so violently to life
at four in the morning, I asked for a story,
so you told me about your pet rabbit from your childhood
who ate so much she made herself sick.

## Catullus Drops a Tab

there were no bugs
crawling under his skin
where that Clodia
had dug her nails in
rather

a procession of sparrows
on the end of the bed
regarding the poet
with all-too-familiar eyes

## High Functioning

I'm being eaten by my feelings
face down in the mud
like a farmer with a brain aneurysm
surrounded by piglets

face down in the mud
nudged and kneaded
hither! the scoffing piglets
me?

fat pheasant flushed from the thicket
nudged and kneaded
tossed mid-air between kārearea
flat present smushed under a winglet

ex-lab-rat on pingers on a treadmill
receiving Aro Park autopsy by absent-minded accipiter

like a farmer with a brain aneurysm
chewed by swine and birds and rodents
I'm being eaten by my feelings

## Killers

    I.

Every summer they put up the signs saying NO FIRES
and every summer, we ignore them.

The sky above the ranges was going shy,
blushing and hiding in the skirts of the hills.

We walked the beach in search of dry driftwood and kindling,
brushing hands but never really holding on.

I had a guitar slung over one shoulder, remembering
an evening long ago when my sandals had washed off the rocks,

the look on my mother's face when I returned after dark,
feet and cheeks marred with tears.

After that summer, *The Walrus and the Carpenter*
became my favourite Carroll piece. Hindsight

had just revealed this correlation when you swung
a warm, sunburnt arm around my waist,

but that wasn't what made me stop.

II.

Their movements melted the mirror of the bay.
Each ripple gave away the bulk hidden beneath.

The two fins offshore gently reminded us
why you don't swim alone at dusk

before slipping behind the islands
like slipshod yachts out in a southerly.

We took it as a good omen and piled the bonfire high,
offering burnt marshmallows as votives to slippery gods

who can knock seals from ice floes
by making waves in military formation.

## Holiday, then

Yes, but I don't fancy it very much.
The sun is much too bright and the water is much too cold.
And the sand gets into everything –
books, bags, bottles . . . bikinis.
And the beach is so noisy every day
with all the screaming children.
It makes it very difficult to concentrate
on my book, sir. Maybe they could extend
your lifeguard duties to include noise control?
Oh, I'd be most appreciative. Can you imagine
how lovely this place would be if it weren't so crowded?
Oh, I should like that very much. The whole place to myself,
now that is my idea of a nice holiday.
You though, you can stay right there.
Don't move. You're keeping my face in the shade.
It must be an awful heavy weight
on your shoulders, sir, knowing
that at any moment
someone might overestimate their abilities and swim a little too far out.
And maybe they don't know how to ask for help?
Maybe they're out there and
you look away for just one second and
    the sea silently swallows them.

## My Father Dreams of His Father
*For J. L. Jardine*

My father dreams of his father
walking in the garden of the old family homestead at Kawaha Point.
I have not been back since he passed away.

As decrepit dogs wander off under trees
to sniff out their final resting places,
elderly men wait in the wings
rehearsing exit lines.

I'm sure my grandfather never envied his dog more
than during those last days.
I'm sure, given the choice, he would have preferred
to slip away under the magnolias.

The garden is tended by different hands now.
My grandmother still walks by the lake,
her little dog in tow. The current man of the house
is more interested in the chasing of swans

than the cultivating of camellias.

My father dreams of his father
walking in the garden of the old family homestead at Kawaha Point.
I have not been back since he passed away.

## For the Rose Garden

when the man came with the trailer of logs I did not understand
the rose garden needs boxing in said mum said dad

punching petals from flowers with hidden hooks seemed an unfair sport
when they laid the logs in a square around the roses I did not understand

but I liked the gravel path down the middle and the big urn on the plinth
at the centre of the square     cold and ugly
like the rest of the bottom of the garden

when we went to a big shed in the country I did not understand
why the man who came to meet us was holding several stumpy feather mops

which were actually six young hens being held upside down by their feet
when we asked him for a box he did not understand

while dad was driving home I did not know what to call them
my siblings and I named two each     Puddles Kat Blonde Bigga and     and

Babs    and    five chickens peer upwards     the sixth one    Sits
when we get home we put the box on the grass and

they understand     the garden is ruined said dad
each border blurred out by the flicking of idle feet except

for the rose garden lined with logs

when I am sad on Sundays and I do not know why
we make for the roses around the urn

kneeling in the wet grass and carefully placing my hands
I roll one log over and jump back

slaters millipedes spiders with egg sacs     afternoon
tea for sturdy hens     Bigga gets first pick

# Things That Spooked the Ancient Romans

*Etenim dirae, sicut cetera auspicia, ut omina, ut signa, non causas afferunt, cur quid eveniat, sed nuntiant eventura, nisi provideris.*

As a matter of fact, frightening events – as well as auspices, omens and signs – do not cause what happens, but they do foretell what will happen unless you are careful.

    Cicero, *De Divinatione* 1.16.29

I.

earthquakes    meteors    eclipses    lightning    storms

an ox climbs to the third storey of a house and then panics
a baby cries 'triumph!'    a wolf steals a sentry's sword
hot springs run with blood
the sea is on fire    a cow gives birth to a colt    a woman turns into a man
a pig is born with a human face
a child is born with the head of an elephant while it rains milk
four statues at the sacred grove of Feronia in Capena sweat blood

mice nibble the gold in a temple of Jupiter    mice gnaw on a golden wreath
harvest grain appears blood-stained    a pig is born with two heads
the altar of Neptune sweats    wasps colonise the temple of Mars
bees take over the Forum    chickens hatch with three legs
the consul's ox warns its master 'Rome, be on your guard'

a four-legged snake is seen    three suns shine at once
a boy with two heads is born
a crested serpent appears at Lanuvium and Caere
and in Campania, there is ample evidence that a cow has spoken

fish are reaped from the fields
ravens pick the gilding from statues and eat it
Capua is covered in locusts    a colt is born with five feet

                    meadows sink into the earth
          stones fall from the sky     a statue of Hercules grows hair
                       laurel grows on a warship
            a pig is born with a human head     milk flows in the river
      two oxen climb onto the roof of a house in a fashionable neighbourhood

                  a kite snares a weasel in the temple of Jupiter
                     and drops it on the heads of the senators
          sacred chickens fly the coop and make new lives in the Laurentian Forest
              a swan glides into the temple of Victory – no one can catch it
                crows put pieces of tile before the feet of Tiberius Gracchus
        an owl cries on the Capitol     it rains milk for three days     a dog speaks
                     a dog eats a banquet set out for a goddess
                         a statue of Mars stands on its head
               black snakes dance on an altar     a woman vomits wheat
            a cow swims through a naval battle to present itself for sacrifice

II.

a human head is found while digging temple foundations
    (here will be the head of the world)
blood flows from the altar of Jupiter
    (victory is coming)
a baby girl is born with a full set of teeth
    (she will bring disaster wherever she goes)
a stolen column is struck by lightning
    (victory for the Romans)
the statue of Apollo at Cumae weeps
    (success for Romans and sorrow for Greeks)
a cow speaks
    (danger)
a rain of meat
    (bloodshed)

honey flows from an altar
    (disease)
milk flows from an altar
    (famine)
Helvia and her horse are struck by lightning
    (dishonour to the Vestal Virgins and the equestrian order)
a flame springs from earth to heaven
    (a brave and handsome man is coming to take charge of the government)

a palm tree grows from an altar of Jupiter
    (victory and triumphs)
the statue of Mars sweats
    (danger and stress – Hannibal is coming)

the wind knocks down a column and a golden statue
    (death to all priests and magistrates – they decide to abdicate)
two black snakes invade Minerva's temple
    (citizens will die)

Mt Aetna explodes, scattering fire and dead fish
    (trouble)

lightning strikes a temple of Jupiter
    (the annihilation of the haruspices and their children)
part of a wall collapses at Pisaurum
    (trouble)
mice gnaw on shields at Lanuvium
    (a very sad thing)
the sound of a trumpet is heard in the air
    (a new breed is born)
a forty-nine-day-old infant speaks
    (and foretells ruin)

a woman gives birth to a snake
    (defeat)
    the snake is thrown in the river, and swims away upstream

a sparrow carries a grasshopper into the temple of Bellona
    (conflict between landowners and the urban population)
swallows make their nest in the tent of a king on campaign
    (defeat)
a dead man points towards Athens
    (Sulla will be victorious)
lightning strikes the statues of Jupiter and Romulus
    and the tablets of the laws
    (bloodshed, fire, end of law, civil war, the empire and the city's fall –
    Catiline wants it all)
lumps of iron rain down
    (wounds will come from above)
a calf is born by the roadside with its head stuck to its leg
    (a new leader for the human race is coming, but they will not be strong
    or secretive)

a mule gives birth
> (death of respectable citizens, the laws will change,
> and matrons will deliver shameful offspring – enter, the war
> of Caesar and Pompey)

a soldier and his war-horses are killed by a lightning bolt
> (a military expedition must be abandoned)

a tree near Cumae sinks into the ground
and its branches remain sticking out
> (A Sibylline oracle predicted
> *internecionem hominum fore,*
> *tantoque eam maiorem quanto propius*
> *ab urbe portentum factum esset –*
> 'the nearer to the city this sunken tree
> the greater the massacre will be –
> a slaughter of human beings')

III.

a child of indeterminate sex is born

a child of indeterminate sex is born as large as a four-year-old
    (the haruspices call it a terrible omen)
    the child is put into a wooden chest and thrown into the sea

a child of indeterminate sex is born among the Sabines,
and a sixteen-year-old is found, likewise of indeterminate sex
    (nature is out of order)
    the children are immediately thrown into the sea

a twelve-year-old child of indeterminate sex is discovered in Umbria
    (abhorrent)
    the senators order that the child be put to death

a child of indeterminate sex is born at Luna
    (plague)
    the child is thrown into the sea

a child of indeterminate sex is born
    (civil strife – Tiberius Gracchus is dead)
    the child is thrown into the river

a child of indeterminate sex is born
    (more children will be born just the same)
    the child [. . .]

a child of indeterminate sex is born
    [. . .   ]
    the child is thrown into the sea

an eight-year-old child of indeterminate sex is found in the countryside
    [ . . .   ]
    the child is thrown into the sea

a ten-year-old child of indeterminate sex is found
    [ . . .   ]
    the child sinks [ . . . ]

weapons seem to clash in the sky and [ . . .         ] is found
the haruspices order [ . . . ]
    [ . . . ]

a sound comes from the depths of the earth and [ . . .         ]
    (scarcity and famine)
    [ . . . ]

a child of indeterminate sex [ . . .     ]
    [ . . . ]
    [ . . .   ] taken [ . . .   ]

a child of indeterminate sex [ . . .     ]
    [ . . . ]
    [ . . .         ] sea

a child of indeterminate sex is born in Urbinum
    [ . . . ]
    [ . . .   ] carried out [ . . . ]

two children of indeterminate sex are discovered
    [ . . . ]
    [ . . .   ]

## Eurydice & the No
### *or How Eurydice Died of Negligence and a Phonetic Misunderstanding*

Orph had charmed the rocks and stones.
The wood's inhabitants came to cut shapes on the dance floor,
lately reclaimed from the ground below,
pressed neatly into place
like the frown on Eurydice's
fierce little face

'No, stop it, no,' she said succinctly, 'I'm recently married, so
get your hands off me.'
As if the mention of Orpheus would make this satyr desist.
He knew, as well as she did, that Orph was busy
building a song to keep the fairy lights on.
Plus, he was feeling the vibe tonight,
and the cry of 'another one please, Orph,'
couldn't go unanswered, groomed as he was
for this exact capacity.

Eurydice, frustrated, wonders who invited the satyrs.
Didn't she say to the planners, 'No rapists'?
Maybe her sanction had been overruled?
To not invite divines would seem quite rude.
At least with the gods, she might get a gift.
Instead, she's stuck with this satyr prick.

Orpheus is playing what sounds like *Wonderwall*
with an augmented fourth chord.
Yet still, the naiads are frothing for him.
Eurydice is used to this sort of thing.
And so, she dances where his eyes can find her,
but her instep seems to encourage the satyr.

He grinds up behind her during a quiet number.
Orph frowns at the fretboard
and lifts one finger

to solo excruciatingly well
but completely miss Eury's desperate looks.
A faun nearby stamps his hoof and says
to his friend, 'Should we have a word?
He's making us bipedal goat-men look bad – oh dear,
I think there's a flute in his pocket –'
Eurydice hears.

She starts to run. The dancers notice.
More Orpheus for them ('Let her go, man.')
She runs through the tables
and under the lights.
No one wants to ask why, because
it might be about becoming a wife
and who wants to have that conversation?
Not this nymph, nor that one.
So, Eurydice runs, and
the satyr chases.

She thinks about Daphne
but she doesn't much fancy forever as a tree.
Plus, Orpheus could still tell her what to do.
Best not go botanical or mineral.

Repugnant with rapaciousness
each tiny hairy leg throbs for the chase.
The flashing white of the soles of her feet
like the tail of a rabbit racing through the wheat.
The music from the wedding, now bride-less, grows faint.
Eurydice begins to cry and wail.
'Please gods, no no no, no no!'
And somewhere, Zeus, scratching his sack,
mishears the girl but shrugs and obliges.
Eurydice trips into a nest of vipers.

She's dead before she knows she's dead,
tumbling through the black onto a nice soft bed.
Persephone extends a silvery hand
and strokes her forehead softly,
'Tough night, little one? You are dead.'
Persy succeeds at appearing benign.
It's not often Hades is graced by a bride.
The queen thought she had better make an effort –
these sorts of ghosts can be quite difficult.
But, to Persephone's quiet surprise,
Eurydice smiles back immediately
and begins to cry with relief.

Something to know about the Grecian language,
and the fauna of the mainland.
The *vipera ammodytes*, meaning 'diver of the sand',
is a venomous specimen called the horned viper,
or, if you were in a hospital in Greece,
having been bitten by a 70-ish-centimetre snake
with a horn above its rostral scale,
you would say '*ochiā!*' as your tissues dissolve
which sounds a lot like *ōchi*, the Greek word for 'no'.

# Notes

### soy boy
'the world is at least fifty percent terrible' was first published in *Starling*. The poem takes its name from Maggie Smith's 'Good Bones' (Tupelo Press, 2017).
'overshoot' was first published in *Starling*.
'how to make toast' was first published in *Starling*.
'bioremediation' was first published in *Minarets' ANNEXE*. Information about Mt Victoria's Innermost Gardens can be found here: https://www.naturespace.org.nz/groups/innermost-gardens
'the president of the united states of america is crazy' was first published in *Starling*.
't/w: dsh' was first published in *Starling*. Information about the Youth'12 survey can be found here: https://www.fmhs.auckland.ac.nz/en/faculty/adolescent-health-research-group/youth2000-national-youth-health-survey-series/youth2012-survey.html
'roy g. biv' was first published in an earlier form as 'red, orange, yellow, green, blue, indigo, violet' in *elsewhere*.
'mariner_1.txt' was first published in *Sponge*. Mariner 1 was supposed to be the spacecraft for NASA's first interplanetary mission but exploded not long after launch due to a coding fault that Arthur C. Clarke dubbed 'the most expensive hyphen in history'.
'current mood' was first published in *Mimicry*.
'the great pumpkin war' was first published in Salty x Foodcourt's *Haunts* zine.
'improvise / adapt / overcome' was first published in Foodcourt's *Verb Journal*.

If you are feeling mentally unsafe, or considering suicide, you can free-call or -text 1737 at any time for support from a trained counsellor. For people aged between 18 and 25 and in the Greater Wellington region, Piki https://piki.org.nz/ offers free personalised therapy.

If you are in a crisis, call 111, or Lifeline on 0800 543 354. People love you.

### What She Sees from Atop the Mauga
'Native Rivalry' was winner of the 2015 NEW VOICES – Emerging Poets Competition.
An earlier version of 'Vinyl Sundays' first appeared in *Ika*.
'docket dates' first appeared in *Potroast*.
An earlier version of 'Mā' first appeared in *Exploring Multicultural Poetry: Accessible, Meaningful Activities to Inspire Young Poets and Poetry Readers* (Essential Resources, 2020).
'Weekend Idol' was first heard on *Six Pound Sound*.

'Chipped China' first appeared in *Blackmail Press*, then in *Best New Zealand Poems 2017*.

An earlier version of 'SkyCity Scraps' was first heard on *Six Pound Sound*.

An earlier version of 'Satellite' first appeared in *Blackmail Press*.

'Parousia' first appeared in *Blackmail Press*.

'Jack Didn't Build Here' was published in *Landfall*.

'The Artistry Effect' first appeared in *Blackmail Press*.

'Maker' was first heard on *Six Pound Sound*.

'My Vā' was performed in the theatre production *Upu Mai Whetu: Mea Fou*.

### The Temple of Your Girl

Part 3 of 'A Gift to Their Daughters' was published in *Landfall*.

'The Flower Crown of Sulpicia' first appeared in *Starling* Issue 3. Sulpicia is the only woman writer of classical Latin poetry whose work survives. As the daughter of the jurist Servius Sulpicius and the niece of Messalla, a military general and patron of literature, Sulpicia is quite clear about her high expectations of her lover, Cerinthus. She wrote during the Augustan period and her work was transmitted from antiquity in the same collection as Tibullus (c. 60–19 BCE).

'Ode to Goon' was published in 'The Friday Poem' on *The Spinoff*. This poem also appeared in *Mimicry* and *Salient*.

'Killers' first appeared in *Starling*.

'My Father Dreams of His Father' was published in 'The Friday Poem' on *The Spinoff*.

'Things That Spooked the Ancient Romans' is a poem constructed from the records of 'prodigies' or odd events that occurred in ancient Rome. Often these prodigies required public religious rites of purification (*lūstrātiō*) to ward off the bad things they foretold and to placate the gods, whose anger was considered the cause of the prodigies. In these records there is evidence to suggest the ancient Romans viewed people of indeterminate sex (whom we refer to today as intersex) as monstrous and killed them in order to keep peace with the gods. The texts I consulted when writing this poem were Livy's *Ab Urbe Condita*, Pliny's *Natural History*, and the 'other' Livy's *Book of Prodigies*. The views expressed in the poem are not my own. The poem first appeared in *Starling*.

'Eurydice & the No *or How Eurydice Died of Negligence and a Phonetic Misunderstanding*' was the winner of the OrphEus Young Writers Competition and was published on The New Zealand Dance Company's website.

**Rhys Feeney** is a high-school teacher and volunteer mental health worker in Te Whanganui-a-Tara. He has a BA (Hons) in English literature as well as an MTchLrn (Secondary) from Victoria University of Wellington. His poetry has previously appeared in *ANNEXE, elsewhere, Mimicry, Sponge, Starling* and various zines. He tweets occasionally at @rhysfeeneybot

**Ria Masae** is an Auckland-based writer, poet and spoken word artist. Her work has appeared in publications such as *Landfall, Ika, takahē* and *Manifesto Aotearoa: 101 Political Poems*. She won the 2015 NEW VOICES – Emerging Poets Competition and the 2016 Cooney Insurance Short Story Competition. Her poems have been published on the Mexican poetry website *Círculo De Poesía*, as well as in the *Best New Zealand Poems 2017* anthology. In 2018, Ria became the Going West Poetry Slam champion, and in 2019 she was a recipient of the NZSA Mentor Programme.

**Claudia Jardine** is a Pākehā/Maltese poet and musician who was born in Te Tihi-o-Maru and grew up in Ōtautahi alongside a suburban menagerie of animals and bugs. She holds a Bachelor of Arts in classics with First Class Honours, from Victoria University of Wellington, and will soon be completing her Master of Arts in the same subject. Her writing has been published in *Starling, Mimicry, Landfall, Sport* and several zines. Her debut indie-folk EP *North* is available on most major music streaming services. In her spare time she plays centre-back for the university women's football squad, or reads.

First published 2020
Auckland University Press
University of Auckland
Private Bag 92019
Auckland 1142
New Zealand
www.press.auckland.ac.nz

© Rhys Feeney, Ria Masae, Claudia Jardine, 2020

ISBN 978 1 86940 921 0

A catalogue record for this book is available from the National Library of New Zealand

This book is copyright. Apart from fair dealing for the purpose of private study, research, criticism or review, as permitted under the Copyright Act, no part may be reproduced by any process without prior permission of the publisher. The moral rights of the authors have been asserted.

This book was printed on FSC® certified paper

Design by Greg Simpson
Printed in Singapore by Markono Print Media Pte Ltd